The Quiet Eye

THE QUIET EYE

A WAY OF LOOKING AT PICTURES

Selected and Introduced
by Sylvia Shaw Judson

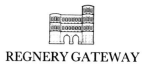

REGNERY GATEWAY

Who loves the rain,
And loves his home,
And looks on life with quiet eyes,
Him will I follow through the storm,
And at his hearth-fire keep me warm;
Nor hell nor heaven shall that soul surprise
Who loves the rain,
And loves his home,
And looks on life with quiet eyes.

Frances Shaw

FOREWORD

When *The Quiet Eye* first appeared in 1954 it pleased and delighted Quakers but it also appealed to a far wider audience. Although quickly reprinted it has been out of print for many years, since when people have never stopped asking for it in bookstores, libraries, and from friends who might have a copy to spare. Now at last it is available again, almost identical to the original but in a smaller format and with many more of the pictures printed in color. Because it is little and easy to carry around it is even better than the original as a picture book to think about and to keep by you.

My mother Sylvia Judson joined the Society of Friends because she was attracted by their simplicity, honesty and personal mysticism, although as an artist she was much bothered by their official unconcern for art. Since the seventeenth century Quakers in their unadorned meeting houses have viewed art with some alarm, as a frill or even a temptation. My mother set out on a one-woman campaign to change this Quaker prejudice by demonstrating that pictures can bear witness to the meaning of intense but quiet words.

Sylvia Judson believed sincerely that the visible outward form truly expresses the spirit within, and she applied this belief to her sculpture, to the way she lived and to the making of *The Quiet Eye*. The book was dedicated to her mother, a poet, and as her daughter I am immensely glad that it is once again available to all the people who have been asking for it as well as to those who will discover it for the first time. I believe that it is needed more than ever today, as a way into meditation and a testimony to the enormous importance of small and quiet things.

Alice Ryerson

INTRODUCTION

THIS book is not meant to teach. It is intended as an experience. The illustrations represent a long and happy search. They are admittedly the choice of one woman who is conditioned by her own life.

Kant defines art as 'the communication of a state of mind'. Plato holds that a work of art exists in its own right: 'not images of beauty, but realities'. These two premises are the basis of the division of art today into the schools of Realism and Abstraction. But one need not necessarily choose between them. A work in either idiom can evoke the same state of mind, or it can be visually satisfying without reference to its meaning.

I hope that these pictures exist as works of art in Plato's sense. The reason that they are in this book, however, is because they communicate a sense of affirmation, of wonder, of trust. This is a spirit alien to much of the art of our insecure time, but one which I am confident will some day return.

I have wanted particularly to find examples with a sense of 'divine ordinariness', a delicate balance between the outward and the inward, with freshness and a serene wholeness and respect for all

1

simple first-rate things, which are for all times and all people. Perhaps these qualities have special significance for me because I am a Quaker. Their flavor, however, is not uniquely Quaker but is implicit in all Christianity although sometimes lost under much cumber.

Those who are searching for spiritual values today seem more inclined to turn to music than to art. Because of its abstract nature, a musical work may be religious in intention without being identified with historic symbols, which many people, raised in a secular age, find limiting. But a picture may also be religious without having a conventional religious subject.

Members of the Society of Friends have traditionally held art in distrust, and that deserves some explanation because so often religion and art have gone hand in hand. Quakerism sprang up in England toward the middle of the seventeenth century. At this time most painting was elaborate and trivial, and the lace ruffles and bows which a man wore in life were reproduced in effigy on his tombstone. It was inevitable that a group sensitive to fundamental social values and of a faith described later by William James as a 'religion of veracity based on spiritual inwardness' should react against such an art.

But Friends, too, accept themselves as whole human beings, and surely it is not a sign of depravity to laugh with Chaucer or to enjoy Rubens. The Reformation left many people indifferent and illiterate in matters to do with art. Anything that can add so immeasurably to our awareness and brings us deeper intuitions is surely worthy of our serious attention. The artist serves humanity by feeding its hungry spirit in as real a sense as if he fed its hungry bodies. He needs to be accepted as a useful member of society, otherwise springs of creativity dry up or turn bitter and society is the loser.

2

I am not suggesting that in order to foster art there should be pictures and sculptures in the meeting houses. The plain integrity of most Quaker meeting houses, with their good proportions, quiet color and restful lighting, and the purity of line of their honestly fashioned furniture, are a proof that buildings have meaning, and transmit the spirit of their builders. Those meeting houses are themselves forms of abstract art, where relationships of line, color, and especially of space, convey emotions. When new meeting houses are built, however, I hope that an antiquarian attachment to the past will not result in the reproduction of old models, no matter how lovely, because the architecture of today could be singularly in the Quaker spirit.

'The sun and stars are mine; if those I prize', writes Thomas Traherne. All of us, whatever our economic means, may have our own art collections. This book is in a sense my collection, but if any of the pictures please you they become yours also.

There is another way that even the simplest home may directly enjoy works of art. The Japanese have a custom of setting aside one place in a room suitable for a painting, a piece of sculpture, or a fine example of calligraphy. When they can afford it, they change these with the seasons or with the months. Such a practice might prove a good solution for us in our diminishing living quarters and would serve to keep them uncluttered, and to keep us aware and looking with fresh eyes. In some cities there is now provision for the renting of pictures. This should prove a good way to enjoy and to learn about paintings without large expenditure or hasty commitments.

It has been an adventure exploring the centuries in order to find my examples. In some periods there were so many that I was obliged to make difficult choices. It hurt not to be able, within prescribed limits, to include Giotto, who served God by painting, or the 'august and serene' Piero della Francesca. In other periods the special qualities that I was looking for seemed almost lost, and in some artists, such as Picasso, they appear, and disappear.

Much of the art of our own time is an art of symbol which is in danger of becoming etherealized quite out of this world. I suppose that one reason for this is discouragement with ourselves as human beings, due to the current confusion and distress in the world, or a sense of our unimportance in the face of the incredible extension of our natural horizons. It is also a yearning to speak a universal language. Sometimes an abstract work achieves this aim, but we remain human beings just the same, and living subjects still hold warmth and immediacy for us.

Contemporary artists are most frequently concerned with change and movement, just as our philosophers are concerned with relative values. In the words of Francis Thompson: 'To all swift things for swiftness did I sue; clung to the whistling mane of every wind.' But cannot quiet and serenity be recognized as well as movement? And cannot the validity of relative values be accepted without rejecting those absolute values realized by the great mystics and artists alike in a still moment of overpowering grace? We know that we are creatures, limited by time and space, but we also know that truth, beauty and tenderness are aspects of the absolute.

If those whose tradition has placed the emphasis on spiritual at the expense of aesthetic values could enjoy this book for its aesthetic quality, and those who are usually interested only in aesthetic values could find in it a spiritual quality, I should feel rewarded.

Sylvia Shaw Judson

4

'We apprehend Him in the alternate voids and fullness of a cathedral; in the space that separates the salient features of a picture; in the living geometry of a flower, a seashell, an animal; in the pauses and intervals between the notes of music, in their difference of tones and sonority; and finally, on the plane of conduct, in the love and gentleness, the confidence and humility, which give beauty to the relationships between human beings.'

Aldous Huxley

'True simplicity consists not in the use of particular forms, but in foregoing over-indulgence, in maintaining humility of spirit, and in keeping the material surroundings of our lives directly serviceable to necessary ends, even though these surroundings may properly be characterized by grace, symmetry, and beauty.'

Book of Discipline of the Religious Society of Friends
Adopted by Philadelphia Yearly Meeting, 1927

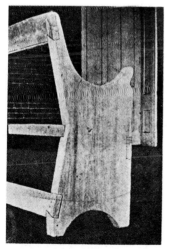

Bench in Stillwater Meeting House

'All things were new; and all the creation gave another smell unto me than before, beyond what words can utter.'

George Fox, English (1624–91)

'Yet all in order, sweet and lovely.'

William Blake, English (1757–1827)

Edward Hicks, American (1780–1849)
The Grave of William Penn

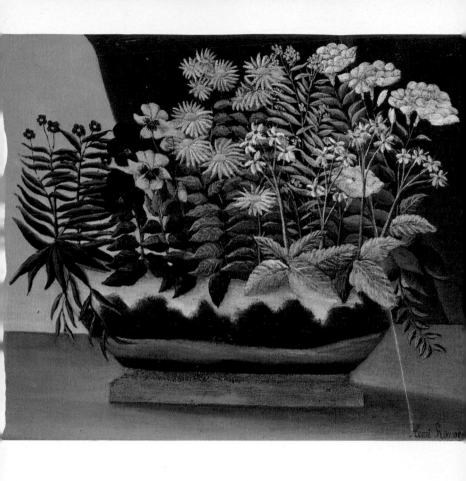

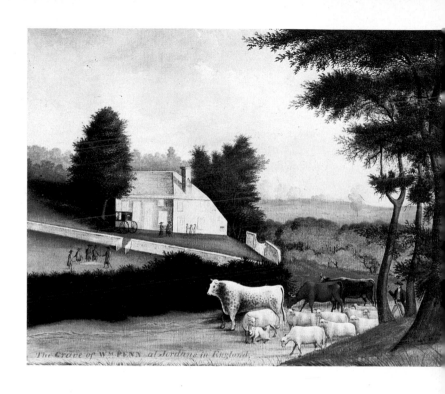

The Grave of Wm PENN at Jordans in England.

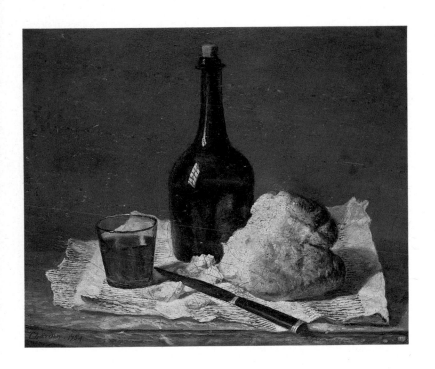

'One eats in holiness

and the table becomes an altar.'

Martin Buber, Israeli (1878–1965)

Follower of Jean Chardin, French (1699–1779)
Still Life

'In a picture I want to say something comforting.'

Vincent Van Gogh

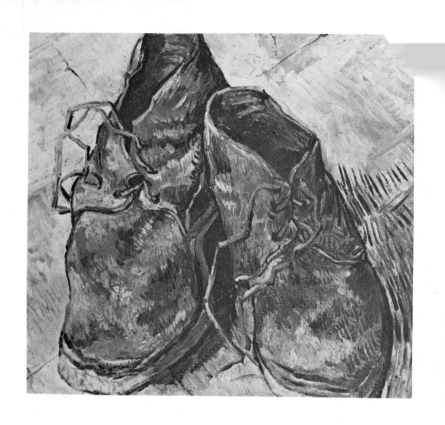

'When you love someone, you love him as he is.'

Charles Péguy, French (1873–1914)

American, artist unknown (c. 1800–25)
Baby in Red Chair

Abby Aldrich Rockefeller Folk Art Center, Williamsburg, Virginia

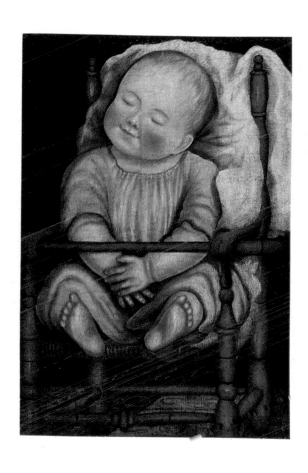

'Give Thy blessing, we pray Thee, to our daily
work, that we may do it in faith, and heartily.'

Thomas Arnold, English (1795–1842)

Vermeer, Dutch (1632–75)
Milk Woman

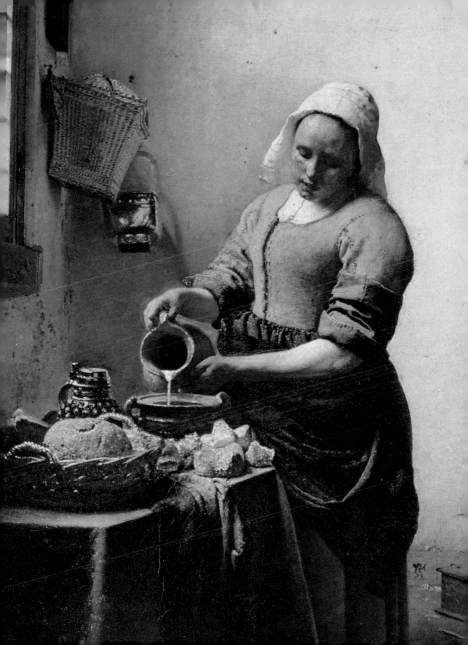

'He came all so still

Where His mother was,

As dew in April

That falleth on the grass.'

Old carol

Georges de la Tour, French (1593–1652)
Le Nouveau-Né
Musée des Beaux-Arts, Rennes

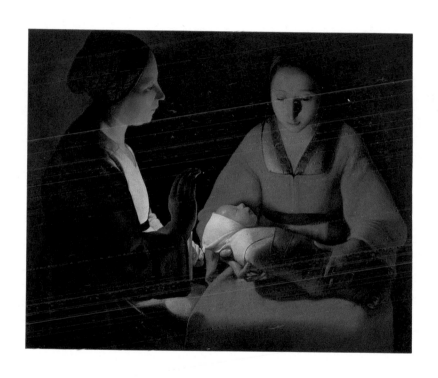

'While the earth remaineth,

seed time and harvest.'

Genesis 8:22

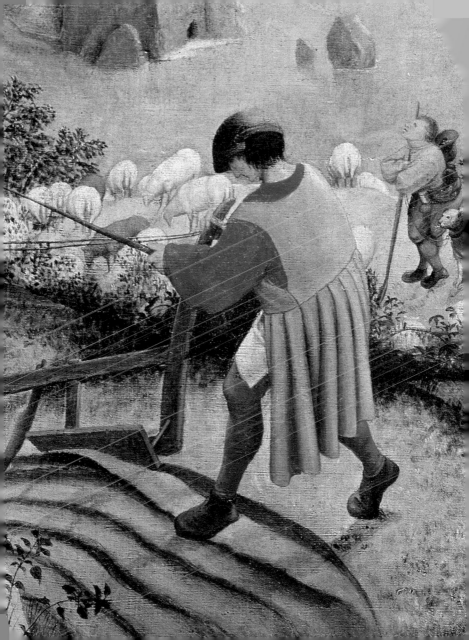

'—a tenderness toward all creatures,'

John Woolman, American (1720–72)

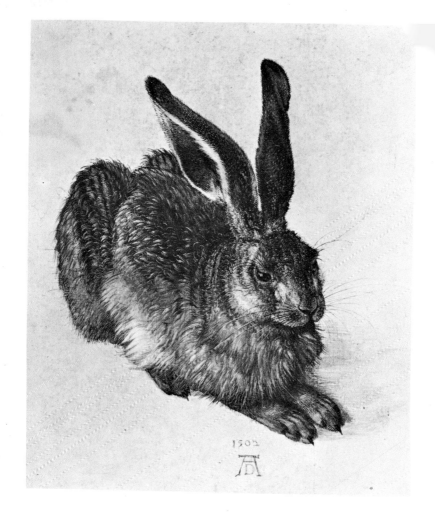

1502

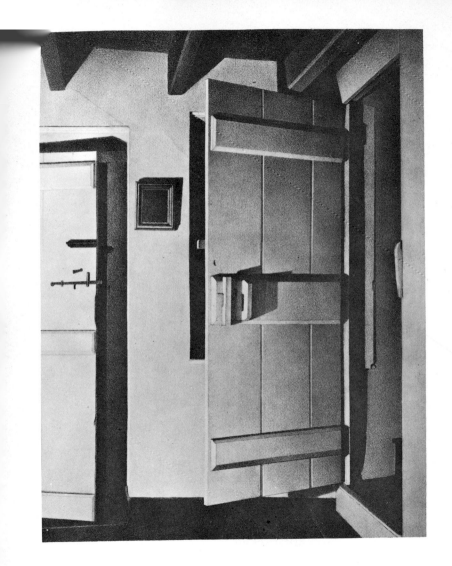

'Things must be right in themselves, and good for use.'

Eric Gill, English (1882–1940)

Charles Sheeler, American (1883–1965)
Open Door

Collection Mr and Mrs Milton Lowenthal, New York

'Feeling light within, I walk.'

Navajo night chant

Indian, from Vancouver, Canada
Private collection

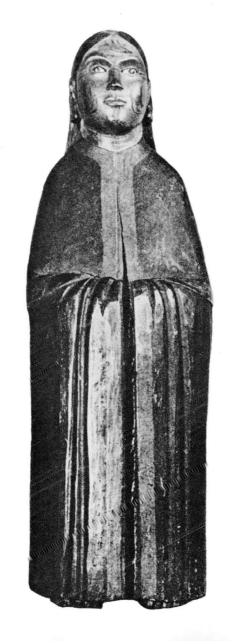

'Thou wilt support us both when little

And even to grey hairs.'

Saint Augustine (AD 354–430)

Henry Moore, English (1898–
Sleeping Child Covered with Blanket, detail
Second Shelter Sketchbook, 1941
The Henry Moore Foundation, Much Hadham, Hertfordshire

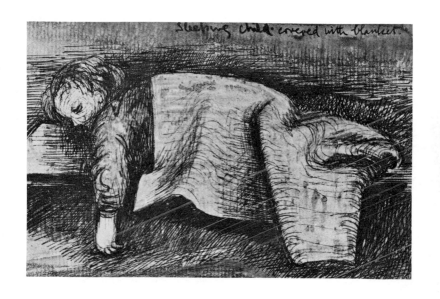
Sleeping child covered with blanket.

'What is all this juice and all this joy?'

Gerard Manley Hopkins, English (1844–89)

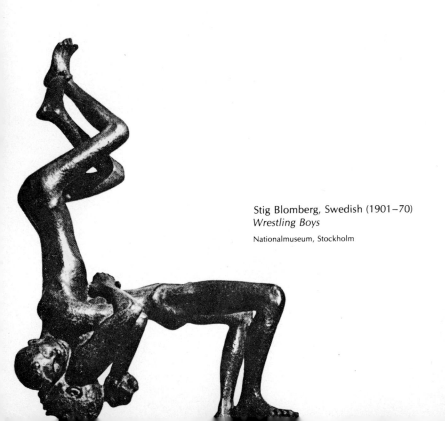

Stig Blomberg, Swedish (1901–70)
Wrestling Boys

Nationalmuseum, Stockholm

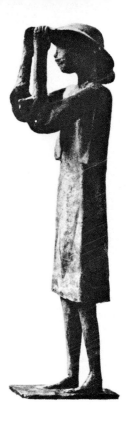

'There lives the dearest freshness deep down things.'

Gerard Manley Hopkins

Hans Wimmer, German (1907–

Private collection

'As to me, I know of nothing else but miracles.'

Walt Whitman, American (1819–92)

Byzantine (4th century AD)
Nativity
Byzantine Museum, Athens
Courtesy Professor George Satiriou

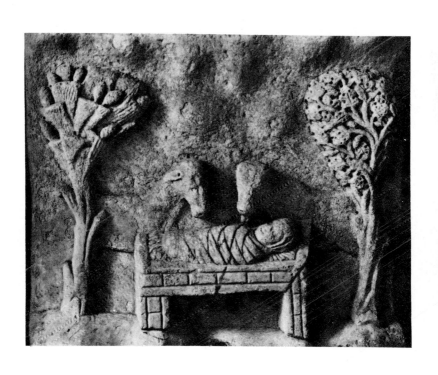

'Father, forgive them

for they know not what they do.'

Jesus of Nazareth, St Luke 23:34

French (12th century)
Christ of the Descent of the Cross
Musée du Louvre, Paris

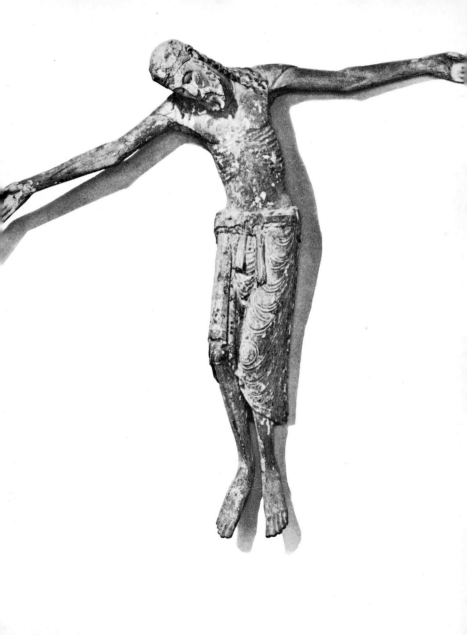

'—but beauty absolute, separate, simple

and everlasting.'

Plato, Greek (428–348 BC)

Constantin Brancusi, Romanian (1876–1957)
The Newborn (1915)
Museum of Modern Art, New York
Lillie P. Bliss Collection

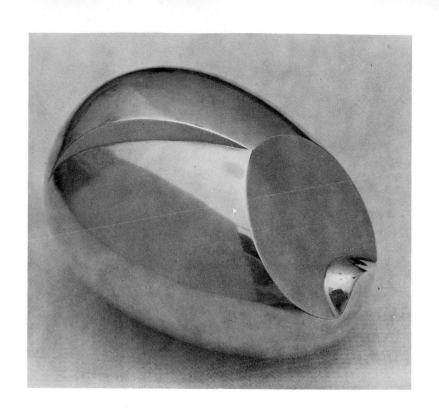

'Thy law is truth

And truth is Thyself.'

St Augustine

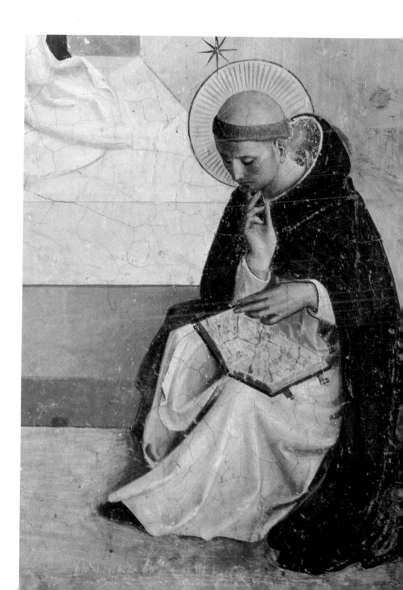

'In simple trust like theirs who heard

Beside the Syrian sea.'

John G. Whittier, American (1807–92)

Duccio, Sienese (1278–1319)
The Calling of the Apostles Peter and Andrew

National Gallery of Art, Washington DC
Samuel H. Kress Collection

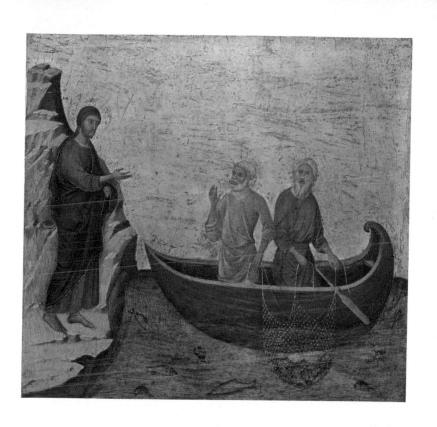

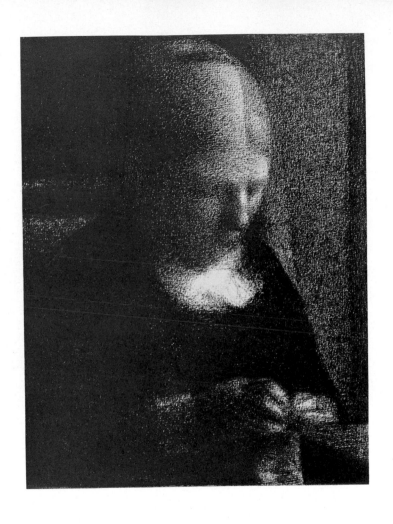

'Great peace is found in little busy-ness.'

Geoffrey Chaucer, English (1340–1400)

Georges Seurat, French (1859–91)
The Artist's Mother

Metropolitan Museum of Art, New York
From the Museum of Modern Art, Lillie P. Bliss Collection

'The way to do is to be.'

Lao Tzu, Chinese (c. 600 BC)

Chang Feng, Chinese (17th century)
Portrait of the Scholar Tu Chun

Courtesy Art Institute of Chicago

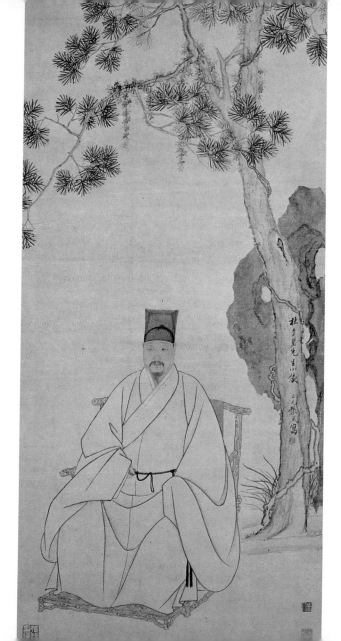

'The sound stops short, the sense flows on.'

Chinese saying

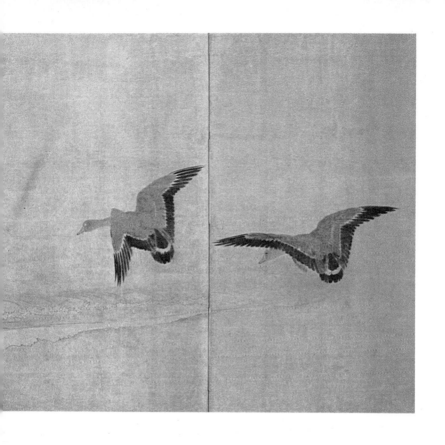

Japanese, Maruyama school (18th–19th century)

'And central peace subsisting at the heart

of endless agitation.'

William Wordsworth, English (1770–1850)

Paul Klee, Swiss (1879–1940)
In Festen Grenzen

Paul Klee Foundation, Kunstmuseum, Bern
(Color plate © COSMOPRESS Genève and ADAGP Paris)

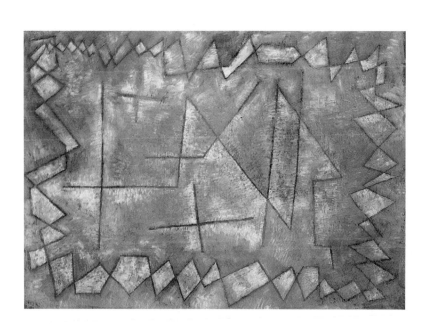

'Work of sight is done.

Now do heart work

On the pictures within you.'

Rainer Maria Rilke, German (1875–1926)

Piet Mondrian, Dutch (1872–1944)
The Tree

Museum of Art, Carnegie Institute, Pittsburgh, Pennsylvania
Patrons Art Fund, 1961

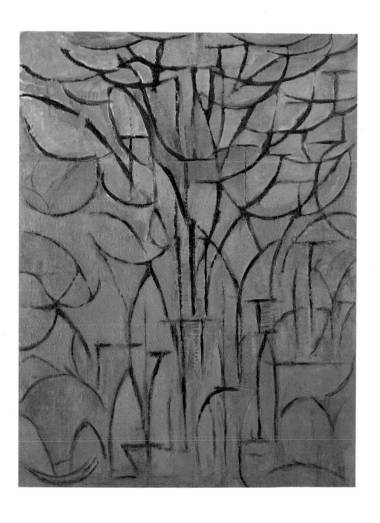

'May the Lord bless thee and keep thee.'

Book of Numbers 6:24

Sassetta, Sienese (1423–50) and assistant
Meeting of St Anthony and St Paul, detail

National Gallery of Art, Washington DC
Samuel H. Kress Collection

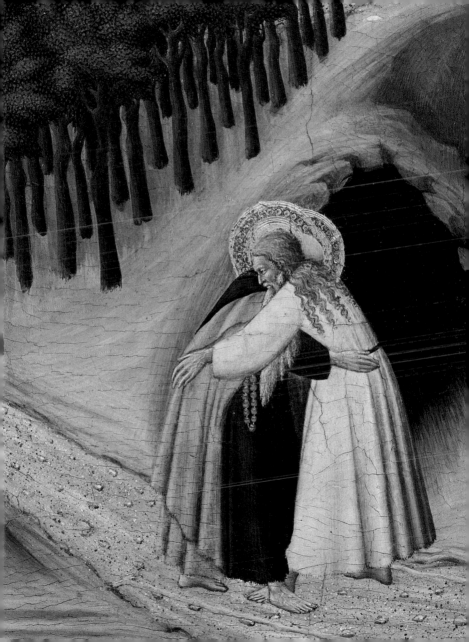

'It is not wisdom to be only wise

And on the inward vision close the eyes.'

George Santayana, born Spain (1863–1952)

Naum Gabo, born Russia (1890–
Linear construction, plastic
Phillips Collection, Washington DC

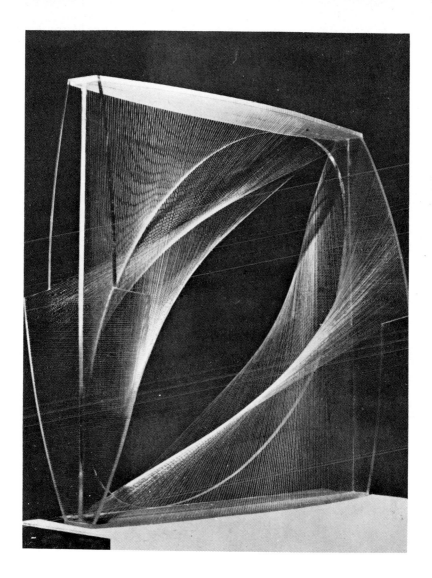

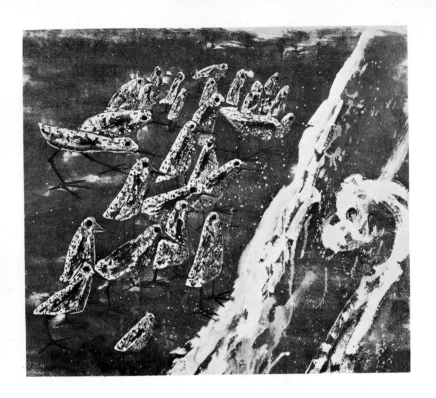

'We are united with all life that is in nature.

Man can no longer live his life for himself alone.'

Albert Schweitzer, German (1875–1965)

Morris Graves, American (1910–
Shore Birds

Collection Lee Foley, Evanston, Illinois

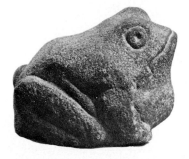

'It's the small things that are hard to do.'

John B. Flannagan

John B. Flannagan, American (1895–1952)
Frog

Courtesy the Detroit Institute of Arts

'Be still and cool in thy own mind and spirit.'

George Fox, English (1624–91)

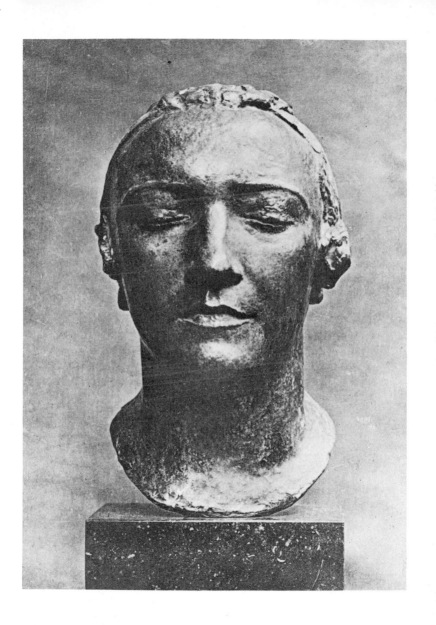

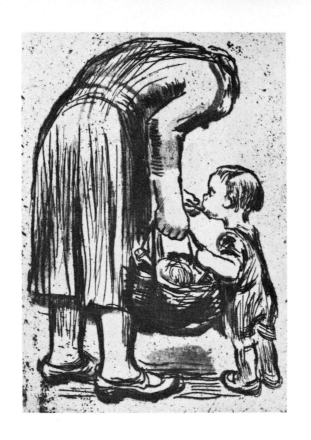

'Caring is the greatest thing,

caring matters most.'

Last words of Freiderich Von Hugel
(born Italy 1852, died England 1925)

Käthe Kollwitz, German (1867–1945)
Home from Market

Verlag Gebr. Mann, Berlin

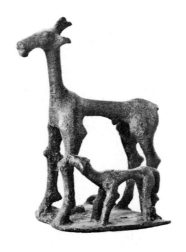

Greek (7th century BC)